Your mind is powerful!
By repeating these affirmations to yourself,
you will start to believe in yourself more and more.
Repeat them to yourself each day
and watch the magic happen!

My words are powerful

I am bold and brilliant

I never give up on my dreams

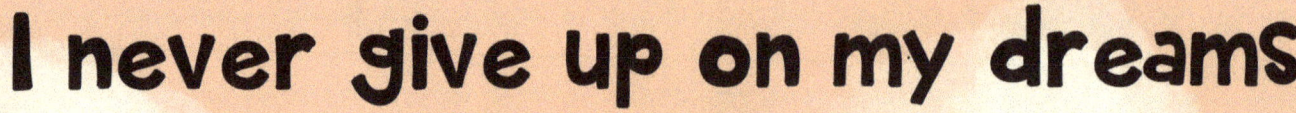

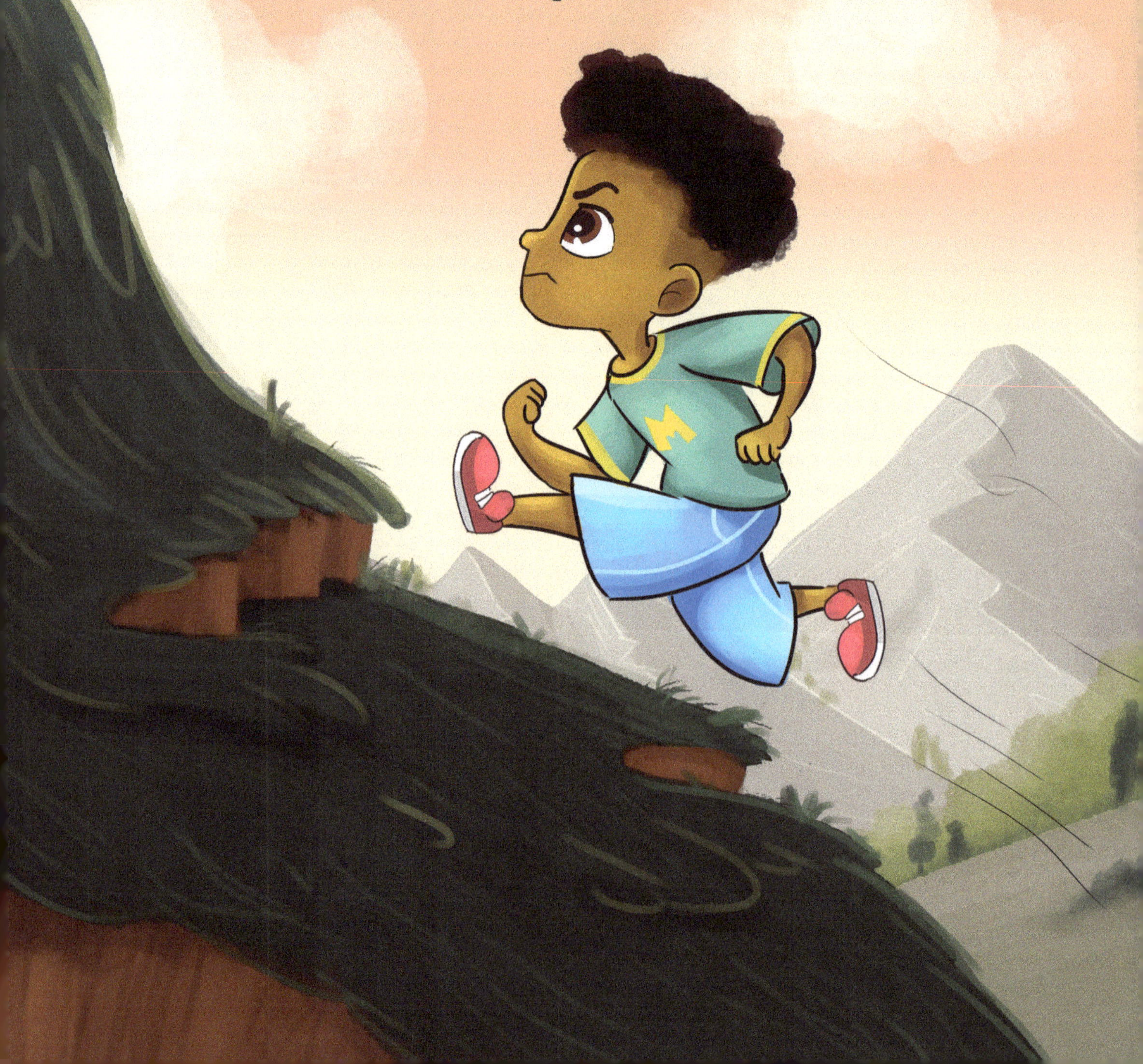

Mistakes help me learn and grow

I am brave enough to try my best

Nothing is too hard for me to figure out

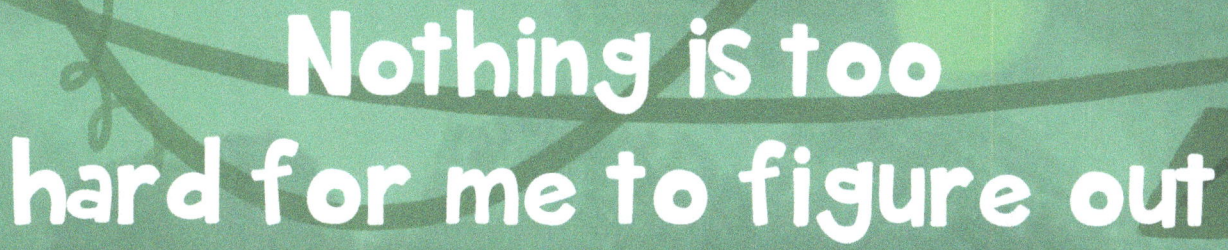

I am kind, curious and creative

I am courageous and confident

I love being me

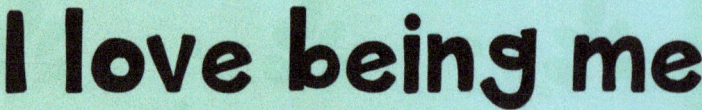

I feel proud of myself when I try new things

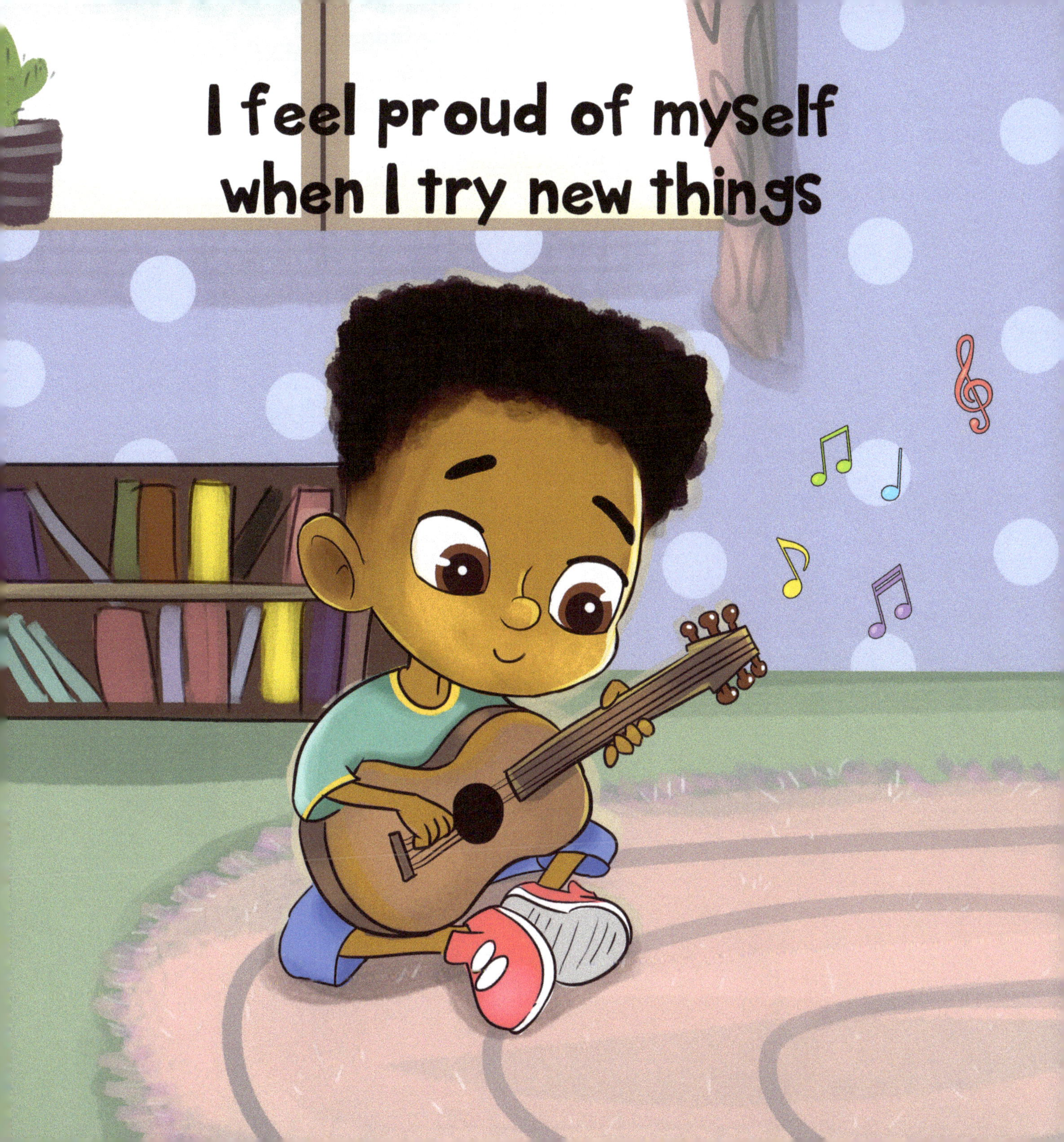

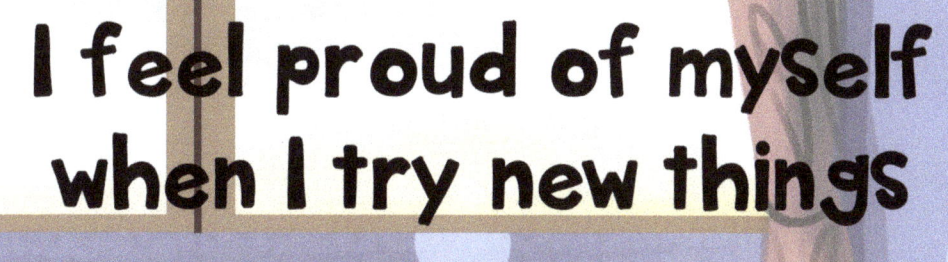

My melanin protects me

My skin is filled with superpowers

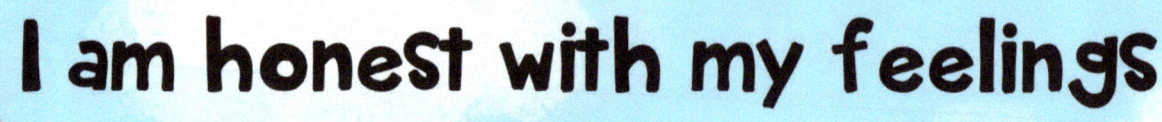
I am honest with my feelings

I enjoy trying new things

I try my best when I try new things

I will make a difference in the world

I can be whatever I want to be

My brown skin makes me beautiful

My best is good enough

I love the skin I'm in

I am brilliant

I am a great friend

I have big, bold dreams

coloring page
with Maverick and friends

www.ingramcontent.com/pod-product-compliance
Lightning Source LLC
Chambersburg PA
CBHW050804220426
43209CB00089BA/1686